INTERVIEWING GRANDDAD

ANDRE PARKER

Copyright © 2022 Andre Parker
All rights reserved
First Edition

PAGE PUBLISHING
Conneaut Lake, PA

First originally published by Page Publishing 2022

ISBN 978-1-6624-7962-5 (pbk)
ISBN 978-1-6624-7963-2 (digital)

Printed in the United States of America

CHAPTER 1

August 20

"Well..."

Arthur sat there, unsure how to ask his grandfather the final question.

"What is it?"

Art was running a little late, which was becoming more commonplace for him. As he pulled into the meeting spot, he saw Jimmy patiently waiting. When he got out of the car, Jimmy smiled at his (now much older than the last time he saw him) grandson.

"I was starting to think you wouldn't show."

"Remind me," Art said as he gathered his pen and notebook, "why aren't we doing this at your house?"

"I didn't want to disturb your grandma again. She deals with me enough as it is."

Art was now standing just a few feet away from his seventy-nine-year-old grandpa. "Wow. You look pretty good for your age!"

"Oh, thanks," Jimmy responded somewhat sarcastically before letting his smile show again. "So are you ready?"

"Whenever you are, Granddad."

Jimmy took a look around before responding. "I've been ready for a while now."

"Great! Let's start simple. State your full name."

"Geez, am I being interviewed or interrogated?" He smiled again.

"Sorry, let me rephrase that. Can I have your full name?" Art paused for a second while readying the pen in his hand. "Please!"

"James H. Parker."

"What does the H stand for? Heinz?"

Jimmy chuckled at this quip. "I could tell you, but I'd rather not. Just think of it like the H that Lewis wrote about."

"I just started reading that book."

"Started?" Jimmy laughed. "It's only four chapters."

"I've been busy."

"What else?"

"Can I get your birthday please?"

"November 28."

"And the year?"

"You know how old I am."

"Granddad, this is the easy part."

"You mean it gets harder? I hope I don't fail."

Art looked up at Jimmy with a smirk on his face. As he made eye contact with his grandfather, they both busted out laughing. After a few moments, they were finally able to compose themselves.

"Oh boy. I've missed this, Granddad."

"Well, if you visited more—"

"I've been busy."

"You keep saying that."

"Because it's true."

"But what if you forget that I exist? Or your grandma? Or your parents?"

"That will never happen."

"Well, for how 'busy' you've been, I wouldn't be surprised."

"I promise you, it won't. I have pictures in my room, on my desk, in my memory, of all of you. Plus, I can always call and hear your voice."

"Okay, okay… I believe you. What's the first 'real' question?"

"So no birth year… I'll ask Grandma later. The first question: what did you do for a living?"

"You don't know?"

"Of course I do, but I can't interview you if I put down the answers in my own words."

"What's this for anyway?"

INTERVIEWING GRANDDAD

"A personal project."

Jimmy stared at his grandson. He could always tell when there was something being kept from him. He was good at that sort of thing. He decided he would let it slide, for now. "I worked my way up the ladder for a local company."

"And the company?"

"Oh jeez, do I need to spoon-feed you everything?"

Art was becoming slightly irritated. "You know, maybe now isn't the best time. I'll come back when you're ready."

"I've been ready."

"Well you aren't acting like it."

"I'm sorry, but it's hard for me to act 'ready' when this is the first time I've seen you in years. No hug, no 'I miss you,' just straight to the interview."

"I didn't think I needed to do those things anymore."

"You don't need to, but you always can."

"Yeah, I was right. You aren't ready for this. I'll come back another day."

Art was becoming more frustrated as Jimmy brought up the past. The only thing he could think to do was get in his car and leave. As he opened the door, he threw the pen and notepad on the back seat.

"Now I'm ready," Jimmy said from the same bench he had been sitting on.

"What?"

"Just don't bring the materials with you. It'll feel more real that way."

Art stood at his car. After pondering for a moment, he decided to see what Jimmy was up to. He closed the door and approached his grandpa, making sure to hug him this time and say the words Jimmy had been waiting for. "I've missed you."

"You know I'm always available, right?"

"Yeah, but I'm not. I've been busy."

Jimmy echoed those last words. "'I've been busy.' I know."

Both men sat in silence for a minute. Both thinking about how they had spent their last few years. One had a lot longer of a list of excuses for not visiting; the other had a lot longer of a list of special moments with loved ones.

Suddenly, Jimmy had an idea. This time with his grandson could be short if he didn't figure out how to stretch it out. So that's exactly what he did. "You keep saying you've been busy. Why don't you tell me what's been going on in your life?"

"Oh, Granddad… I wouldn't even know where to start."

"Why don't you start with telling me why you were late to class?"

Art gulped. "You know about that?"

"Well, of course. All grandparents know everything."

"What do you mean by that?"

"We've lived a lot longer. We've had more time to figure things out."

"Oh…okay. I guess that makes sense."

"Now tell me."

"Tell you what?"

"Why were you late to class?"

The final time Jimmy asked Art this question, he could have sworn he heard Professor Benjamin's voice speak simultaneously with his grandpa's.

CHAPTER 2

Late to Class

"Arthur, are you okay?"

Robert Benjamin was leaving the cafeteria and getting ready to head out for the day, aside from it only being noon, when he noticed Art frozen in place at the entrance to CC (college center) Square.

Students and faculty alike walked past Art as if he was another statue. Some gave him a look, but most just brushed passed him.

Benjamin had taught only one class Art took, but he knew him very well. The two had been a big part of Living in Faith Every Day, LRC's Christian fellowship. He also made an effort to get to know Art personally between lunches and Bible studies.

He could tell that something was off and decided to check in on someone he cared about. As he approached Art, he realized that this was the worst he had ever seen him.

"Arthur, are you okay?

Art stayed frozen for a moment before he realized that someone was talking to him. "Oh, hi, Rob. How long have you been standing there?"

"Long enough." Benjamin paused. "Do you need to talk?"

"I don't know if talking about it will help."

"Talking about what?"

"You know how sometimes you'll think you see someone you know, like in a crowd or something, but when you approach them, it's not them."

"Sure. We all have those moments."

"Well, I just had one."

Benjamin thought to himself for a moment. *Something like that wouldn't normally stop Arthur in his tracks. There must be more to it.* "Why don't we sit down and talk?"

"There are so many people here."

"Then let's go to the tables by the bookstore. There's a lot less people over there."

Benjamin started walking toward the bookstore, turned, and ushered Art to follow him, and the two were off.

With La Roche being such a small school, they were there within fifteen seconds. (And that's even with them going to the farthest table away from CC.)

"So…what's on your mind?"

"The person I thought I saw is someone I haven't talked to in a while."

"Why's that?"

"I'm currently mad at them."

"When was the last time you saw this person?"

"I was seventeen."

"Oh… So it's been a few years. What did they do to upset you so much?"

"He left my family when we needed him most."

"So it's a he? May I ask who?"

"My grandpa."

*****

Art was walking out of the cafeteria and on his way to class. One of his favorites: Charles Edwards' New Testament. He always looked forward to this class.

As he was about to exit CC, he saw an older man leaving the building. He could have sworn it was his granddad Jimmy. He tapped him on the shoulder.

"What are you doing here?"

The man turned around, and it wasn't Jimmy. He had never seen this man before.

"I'm sorry?"

Art stood there, unsure how to answer. "No, I'm sorry. I thought you were someone else."

The stranger continued to walk away. As he walked out of Art's sight, Benjamin was leaving the cafeteria.

*****

"So why haven't you forgiven him yet?"
"He left us."
"Did he have a good reason?"
"You'd have to ask him that yourself."
"Why don't you ask him?"
"Is that the personal project you were referring to?" Jimmy interrupted Art's story.
"It was where the idea first came from, but otherwise, no."

*****

"I'm sorry I left, Arthur. I really am, but everyone else has forgiven me. Your grandma had the biggest reason to be upset, but she forgave me."
"I know she did, but she's a better person than I am."
"Your parents, aunts, uncles, and cousins all forgave me."

*****

"Do you want to hear the rest of this story or not?"
"It's not that easy, Rob. It really changed me when he left."
"For the worse?"
"No...for the better actually."
"Then ask him."
"I'm just not ready for that yet."
"Why?"

As Benjamin and Art continued their conversation, they lost track of time. Before they knew it, classrooms were emptying again.

Art wiped the tears from his face that had formed over the course of the conversation.

"It must be two already."

"Hey, I'm sorry. I didn't mean to make you so emotional."

"It's fine. I actually think it helped."

As Benjamin smiled at Art, another familiar voice came from behind Art.

"Skipping class today, are we?"

Art turned around and saw Edwards standing only a few feet behind him.

"Hey, Charles. It's my fault Art was late today."

"Late? He missed the whole class."

"I'm sorry, Dr. Edwards. It won't happen again. Thanks for the talk, Professor Benjamin. I'll see you both later." Art gathered his materials and headed towards his dorm, still puffy eyed.

"Is he okay, Robert?"

"No, I don't think he is."

"Do I need to talk to him?"

"I think I got it covered for now."

"All right."

As Edwards headed to his office, Benjamin stopped him. "Wait. Before you go, can you give him a chance to make up the classwork? You know I wouldn't ask if it wasn't important."

"You know I like him, Robert. I don't want to see him fail either."

And with that, the two shared a smile and went their separate ways.

Chapter 3

Tuesday Morning

"Hold on. You were failing?"

"That's the funny thing. I wasn't."

"Then why did he say—"

"Because they both wanted to see me succeed in life too."

"That's just an odd thing to hear from your teachers."

"They're college professors, and now they're purely my friends."

"It's a little confusing, that's all."

"What's confusing, Granddad, is leaving your family with no explanation."

"You want an explanation?"

"It probably wouldn't make a difference now."

"You want one? I'll give you one."

"You can try to give me one."

*****

Jimmy woke up earlier than his wife as he did every Tuesday and Thursday morning. Those were his exercise days. He would go to the gym that was only ten minutes away and play tennis for a little while before heading home.

While he would do this, his wife would wake up not long after he left. She would use the time to herself to miss her husband but also enjoy some moments alone.

As was habit, he would always leave the bathroom and bedroom door open so that she knew he was no longer in the house…except for on the day he left.

On that particular Tuesday morning, Jimmy got a call he wasn't quite prepared to answer while he was in the bathroom.

"Hello?"

No one answered.

"Is it time to go?"

Again, no response.

"Let me say goodbye to my wife first."

Jimmy kissed his wife on the forehead and whispered, "I'll be back before you know it."

A few minutes later, she heard her alarm and turned it off. As she got out of bed, she saw that the bathroom door was still closed.

"Jimmy, honey, is everything all right?"

*****

"So you left her while she was sleeping?"

"I didn't have a choice."

"You did."

"No, I really didn't. I had to go."

"But why?"

"I said I'm sorry, Arthur."

"You want to know how I found out?"

"I already know who told you."

"Maybe you heard the story, but not from my point of view."

*****

Art woke up to his phone ringing. *Who is calling me this early?* He grabbed his phone and looked at the time. *Crap. I'm gonna be late to Grandma and Granddad's. Wait, why is Nanny calling me?*

"Hello?"

"Hey, bud. Can you come over and help Poppy for a minute?"

INTERVIEWING GRANDDAD

"I can't, Nan. I'm already running late to Grandma and Granddad's."

"Please. I wouldn't ask if it wasn't important."

"Okay, just let me call Grandma first and—"

"It's an emergency." Nanny interrupted.

"Okay, okay. I'll be over in a few."

Art got out of bed, changed his clothes, and drove the five-minute drive to Nan and Pop's.

Where is Poppy's car? He walked in through the shoppe (Nanny ran a beauty shop out of the side of her house) and asked her where he was.

"He had to run out for a minute, but he'll be right back."

"Oh…okay."

As Art walked around the house, trying to kill time, he saw his aunt and cousin there.

"Hey, what are you guys doing here?"

"Just hanging out. You should join us."

Art sat for a minute but quickly got bored. As he found his way to the dining room, hoping to distract himself, he heard Poppy pull in.

"Hey, bud, can I talk to you outside?"

"Yep, I'll be right out."

He made his way outside and to where Poppy was standing.

"Bud, there comes a time in everyone's life where—"

Arts thoughts interrupted. *Oh no, does he know about my secret. Is he mad at me? Am I in trouble?*

Poppy concluded. "Your granddad is gone."

*****

"Do you know how much it hurt that I found out you left from Poppy?"

"I had nothing to do with that."

"You're the one that left."

"I told you, I didn't have a choice."

"Fine…but I was still upset for a while at Mom."

"Why?"

"Because she didn't tell me either."

"Do you know how hard it was for her to tell your dad? She couldn't do that again."

"How do you know that? You weren't around."

"Because she told me everything."

"Did everyone else talk to you already?"

"Yeah, you're the last one."

"I'm sorry. It shouldn't have taken me this long."

"You have no reason to be sorry."

"But I was frustrated for a long time."

"At me? Or at yourself?"

"I don't know how to answer that. Maybe both."

"Do you remember what happened the last time I saw you?"

"Of course I do. I thought they were my last words to you."

"Well…were they?"

"Not anymore."

"What did you say again?"

Chapter 4

Friday Afternoon

Art had just returned from visiting Washington and Jefferson College with his grandma. When they pulled in, Granddad was doing yard work at the end of the driveway.

Art walked Grandma inside and said goodbye. As he exited, he went straight for his car before stopping and deciding to be a nice grandson. From his car door, the following conversation ensued:

"Goodbye, Granddad. I love you, and I'll see you Tuesday."

"Bye, Arthur. I love you too. See you Tuesday."

*****

"How was I supposed to know that you were going to die just a few days later?"

"You didn't. Nobody did. That's why your last words meant so much to me."

"To you?" Art laughed. "Imagine how they helped me cope."

"Okay, so the cat's out of the bag. You finally admit you're talking to a guardian angel. Did that help you cope at all?"

"Of course not. I still miss you."

"What's the first question again?"

"What?"

"In your notebook. What was the first question?"

"I thought we were past that."

"I think you need a few minutes. So what was the first question again?"

"What did you do for a living?"

"I started as a member of the air force, and then after I met your grandma, I left that to work my way up at Heinz."

"I already knew all that."

"Then why did you ask?"

"To start a conversation."

"I think we are way past the start of a conversation."

"Yeah… I didn't know it could be this easy."

"To talk to your granddad?"

"To talk to my dead granddad."

"I'm not dead. I'm simply just not breathing anymore."

"Isn't that the definition of dead?"

"No, because I still have my afterlife."

"Right, but you did die to get there."

"Only physically."

"Okay."

Art looked around the cemetery for the first time since he had arrived. He noticed that the number of tombstones was much larger than when he was there last.

"You were only seventeen. I don't expect you to fully understand."

"No, I understand. I just miss you."

"I'm always right here."

"If you pull some ET stuff and point at my heart—"

"ET? Is that something Poppy would do?"

"What?"

"ET are his initials, aren't they?"

"No, well, they are, but I meant the movie."

"You know I never watched a lot of movies."

"Yeah, I know."

After a few seconds of silence, Jimmy continued.

"How is Poppy anyway?"

"Better than he has been recently, but not his best."

"I'm sure that's true. Beating cancer twice is not easy on one's body."

"Three times, actually."

"Oh right, he got it again after I passed."

"How do you know that?"
"I'm a guardian angel, that's how."
"So you know everything?"
"Well, not everything."
"What do you mean?"
"If I want to know something, I can find it out, but I don't actively search for answers to everything."
"Why not?"
"There are things we just aren't meant to know."
"Who told you that?"
"Our Father."
"You mean, you've met God?"
"I've been gone for a while, Arthur."
"I know, but still."
"You've met God too."
"I have?"
"Yes. In every breath, in the trees, in your parents. In everything around you, there is God."
"That's amazing. I mean, you always hear it, but now I know it's true."
"You already knew it was."
Art smiled as he looked at the ground.
"Now tell me, how's Poppy?"

Chapter 5
The Big C

For years, I've been trying to figure out what to say to you. I've been hurt by you before, and I don't think that's fair. Not once, or twice, or even three times. You've hurt me far too much for me to count. You've tried to take him away from me over and over again, but you have yet to win that battle. Even when you do, he'll still be the real winner. You don't know how that's possible? Because it's a win-win for him. Sure, you could kill him, but he won't feel pain anymore. You could also let him live, and he'd feel the pain, but he'd be shown yet again that he can do anything and that his family and friends will always be there for him. You can't win! It's impossible. You've given me moments with him that wouldn't have existed without your help, so I should thank you for that. Not just me, but everyone who cares about him, or even who care about who cares about him. The numbers keep rising for those in his corner, and your number stays the same. It's just you. You might be a lot stronger than him, but when we all rally together, we will defeat you. Good luck taking that away from him. Even if you take him out, you'll never knock him down.

    Jimmy looked up from the notebook Art had gone to retrieve from his car's back seat. While he read it, Art took the few minutes to stretch. He sat back down just as Jimmy finished.

    "Arthur, that's beautiful."

    "Another personal project."

    "I bet it wasn't easy to write."

    "It wasn't. The first attempts made me seem angry at God, which I'm not, so I kept trying until I made it as if I was writing the letter to cancer itself."

"I can feel your raw emotions pouring out with every word."
"Thanks!"

Jimmy looked at the notebook again before setting it down. When he looked back at his grandson, he smiled.

"So he's doing better?"
"As good as he can be."
"Does he miss me?"
"They all miss you. You weren't blood related, but Mom's whole side of the family still loves you."
"Grandma says they've been very welcoming."
"They sure have been."
"And Nanny and Poppy just had their sixtieth anniversary, right?"
"That's right. August 12."

Jimmy chuckled. "Your cousin's sixteenth birthday."
"Yep."
"I'm happy for them."
"Me too. There were plenty of times we didn't think he'd make it this far."
"I know."
"Right. 'Cause you know everything."
"I don't, and I don't claim to, but he was like that before I passed too."
"I know," Art paused. "I'm sorry. It's just hard to talk about him sometimes."
"Have you talked to anyone else about him?"

Art smirked. "Are you kidding? He's the thing I talk to anyone about the most."
"Doesn't help though, does it?"
"It didn't help with you, and it doesn't help now."

Jimmy could feel Art becoming upset toward him again.
"Arthur, I'm sorry. But you know I didn't have a choice."
"Yeah, I know."
"Do you? You're making it seem like it was my call."
"I know it wasn't. I'm just hurt about it still."
"Even after all these years?"

"I told you, it changed me."

"For the better."

"Yes, but it still changed me."

"How?"

"What?"

"How did it change you?"

"You mean you don't know?"

"I want to hear your version of it."

"I tried my best to make every last moment count."

"That's a lot of pressure."

"I mean, like when I would go to bed every night while still living with Mom and Dad, I would make sure to tell them goodnight. Even if they were asleep already."

"Did this with Poppy too?"

"Always."

Another thought popped into Jimmy's head. "Do you remember what it was like when Nanny's Mom passed?"

"Of course. She was the first person to die that I was close with."

"She says 'hi' by the way. Anyways, do you remember how much it hurt?"

"Only until you were gone." Art started to catch on to the distraction. "Before you change the subject again, question two. How much did Grandma change your life?"

"Oh boy…that might take me some time to figure out the best answer to. While I think about it, tell me, what was it like for you to lose someone for the first time?"

CHAPTER 6

The Hardest Part of Love

"Is letting go," Art said as he finished expressing what it was like for him to lose someone at fourteen.

"Okay, so it was hard to let go. But how did it make you feel?"

"It obviously hurt."

"Do you remember what I said to you that day?"

"Not really, Granddad."

"Let me remind you."

*****

Art and his parents had just arrived at the Parker family reunion. His mind was barely there as he couldn't stop thinking about that morning.

His great-grandma Blaine was the first loss he could remember suffering. She was ninety years old when she passed away earlier that day.

As they stepped out of the car, he thought about his last few moments with her. All her great-grandchildren, his cousins, had surrounded her hospice bed, holding hands as they sang "Jesus Loves Me" to her.

The family stayed with her until her dying breath. Nanny, Poppy, all their children, in-laws, and their grandchildren stayed in the depressing room on again and off again for the last week.

Suddenly, Art was stopped by Grandma and Granddad.

"She's gone," Mom said with tears in her eyes.

"Awe, I'm so sorry guys," Grandma responded.

"Thanks," Dad said as he went in for a hug.

Jimmy looked over and saw his young grandson wasn't speaking.

"Come with me," he said as he reached his hand out to Art.

Art grabbed it and followed Jimmy to a private space in the shade. They sat down and then laid in the grass, looking up at the sky above.

"Losing someone is never easy, but it's a lot harder when it's your first."

"I miss her."

"I know you do, and you always will."

"Does the pain ever go away?"

"Arthur, the pain will always be there. However, I can tell you that it does subside into almost nothing."

"How is that supposed to help? I don't know that I want it to go away."

"What I mean is, the pain you feel in your heart will be replaced with happy memories. Photos on your phone, your desk, memories you have together. All these things will help you to never forget her."

"But the pain is still there?"

"Sometimes, but it'll go away the more you remember that you'll see them again someday."

"I love her so much!"

"That's the hardest part of loving someone, Arthur. Letting them go."

"I don't want to let her go."

"I know. Just know that when you do let her go, she'll come back. That old adage is true."

"What old adage?"

"If you love someone—"

"Set them free."

*****

Art started to tear up. He had forgotten a lot of what Jimmy had just reminded him.

INTERVIEWING GRANDDAD

"Granddad, I miss you."
"You know I'm only a call away, right?"
"I've been busy."
"You keep saying that. What's been keeping you so busy?"
"Life."
"Wow, that's cryptic."
"I'm sorry. It's just been a while since I've had a lot of free time."
"So why now?"
"Because I've got nothing but time."
"Time isn't real, you know that. Most of it is man-made. God gave us life. We started timing it."

Art whipped the last tear from his face. "Now, can you please tell me?"

"I'm still not ready to answer question 2."
"Why not?"
"Have you met your grandma? I need to really think about how to answer that question. She's done so much for me I don't want to ruin it with a bad answer."
"Okay, fine."
"Hey, how are your aunt and uncle doing?"
"Better. The car accident was scary though."
"I know it was."

Chapter 7
Not Time Yet

Art had just barely woken up on this beautiful early September morning when he got a call from his mom.

His parents had gone to NYC with Grandma while he stayed home to start grad school, an online program but challenging nonetheless, and house-sit.

"Hi, Mom!" He was barely able to talk from how tired he was.

"Artie, sweetie, I wanted to let you know something. J and Z were in a car accident this morning. It was really bad."

"Are they okay?"

"They're alive. That's all I can tell you."

"Okay."

"Call Nanny and see if they need help around the house, would you?"

J and Z were living in an apartment connected to Nanny and Poppy's house at the time of the accident.

"Sure."

"I love you, Artie!"

"I love you too!"

Art wasn't sure if he could call Nanny without freaking out, but he tried his best. He didn't want her to know he was just as worried.

He called their house and waited while the phone rang. Eventually, Nanny answered.

"Hi, bud!"

"Hi, Nan!"

"We're heading down to the hospital soon. Do you want to join us?"

Art was both surprised and relieved that she knew why he was calling. "Not today. I have some things to do here."

"Do you mind checking on our dogs?"

"No, I can do that later."

"Thank you! And if D isn't able to, would you drive us to the hospital tomorrow or Friday?"

"Sure."

"Thanks, bud!" She paused for a second. "I'll be right there!" she yelled to someone else. "Poppy says it's time to go. Love you!"

"Love you too, Nan!"

A few hours later, Art stopped at their house to let their dogs out. When he opened the door, both toy poodles ran for the yard. They stopped when they saw it was him and jumped for joy. Both girls loved him almost as much as they loved Poppy.

"Hello?" a voice came from inside the house as he let the dogs back in.

Art turned and saw his younger cousin, Ro, standing at the top of the stairs.

"Shouldn't you be in school?"

"My friend's mom brought me home early when she heard about the accident."

"Oh, lucky you. Won't you have a lot of work to make up though?"

"It's the first week."

"Good point."

A moment of awkward silence.

"I just let the girls out."

"Okay, I can do it again later."

"Have you heard anything yet?"

"Just that they're in the hospital."

"Okay. I'm going to head home now."

"See you later, dork."

"See you later."

Art went outside, shutting the door behind him, and headed for his car.

It was Art's senior year of high school, just a month before graduation, when J and Z got married.

He was excited because he was asked to be a groomsman. No one had asked him to be a part of their wedding party before.

As they said their vows, he got to stand behind Z. When they had the reception, he got to sit next to them. It meant more to him than they may ever know.

Few months before the accident, they had their five-year anniversary. As a surprise, Art wrote them a letter and got them a few gifts.

"J's like a big sister to me, you know that?" Art explained to his parents.

"So what did you get them?" Dad asked.

"A few small things."

"And what does the letter say?" Mom inquired.

"That's for them to know. It's not your fifth anniversary." Art chuckled while his parents smiled back at him.

A couple of days after the accident, Art went to the scene with H and D, another aunt and uncle, to see if they could find anything that was left.

"They lost her phone and his watch," H said as they dug through the nearby grass.

"Could be anywhere from the intersection to that tree." D pointed fifty or so feet away.

"I hope we can find it for them." Art was silently freaked out by the scene of the crime.

After a few minutes of looking, they couldn't find either item anywhere.

"Should we check the mechanics?" H brainstormed.

"Might as well," D responded.

Art followed them to the car, never wanting to look back.

*****

"D found his watch in the back seat, and I was able to carefully reach in and grab it without cutting myself, but her phone was a lot harder to find."

"But you did find it?"

"Eventually."

"I bet that was scary for you."

"Are you kidding, Granddad? I can't even drive through that intersection without freaking out. I know I wasn't there when it happened, but I saw the images all over the computer and the papers."

"I'm sure it changed you."

"Yeah, it did."

Jimmy could tell that he was unintentionally bothering his grandson.

"Hey, they survived."

Art looked up as Jimmy put his hand on his shoulder.

"I know." Art put his hand on top of Granddad's.

Suddenly, he was reminded of all the times he thought he was going to lose Poppy but didn't.

Chapter 8

The Chicken King

For years, ET owned his own chicken barbeque business where he would serve customers at fairs and farm shows all over the country. His chicken was some of the best you could ever have.

Sadly, he made the decision to stop when he was diagnosed with cancer the first time. His chicken was good, but his family all wanted him around much more than some food.

Years later, between the second and third time, he had to have surgery that had him scared he wasn't going to make it.

As a result, he gathered his whole family in his private hospital room at AGH. He told them all what he wanted them to do if he didn't make it, how much he loved them all, and how he wanted them all to keep an eye on Nanny.

Art was nineteen when this happened. He had just lost Granddad not that long ago, and he was scared it might happen again.

As everyone left the night before the surgery, Nanny, Mom, and Art stayed behind with Poppy. Nanny slept in the extra bed while Mom and Art tried their best to sleep on a few chairs.

When the morning came, they quickly got ready for the day before the nurse came to wheel Poppy off.

"Mr. Taylor, are you ready to go?"

"Can I just have a few moments please?"

"Of course."

The nurses had laid him down on the hospital bed while the conversation took place.

INTERVIEWING GRANDDAD

Nanny was the first in line to say goodbye to Poppy. She kissed him on the lips, with tears in her eyes, as she said "I love you."

Next was Mom. She kissed him on the forehead, tears in her eyes, as she said, "I love you, Dad."

Finally, it was Art's turn.

Art walked up to the bed, dry-eyed as he looked Poppy in the eyes. "I'm not gonna kiss you, Poppy."

Art could hear Nanny and his mom in the background saying something like "Go on and kiss him," but he tuned them out the best he could.

"Well, then take my hand." Poppy was staring back.

For the first time in Art's life, he felt time stop as he grabbed Poppy's hand. Poppy cusped both hands around Art's as they stared into each other's eyes.

In reality, it was probably only about ten seconds, but Art insists that time stopped while the two men stared in silence. Saying everything they wanted to, without a single word.

The nurse eventually interrupted.

"Okay, it's time to go."

Art let go, took a step back, and turned around. As quickly as his head was turned, a single tear became a waterfall. He whipped them away, and when he looked back, all he saw was Poppy's feet as the bed made its last stretch.

A few years after that, in the same hospital, Poppy almost lost his life again. He was moments away from choking to death but was luckily saved just in time.

After he heard this happened, Art gathered two of his closest friends, who were like brothers to him. Inkspot and Big Red, their nicknames, would do anything for Art.

The three went down to the hospital, found his room, and spent an hour just talking with him. Making sure he was okay first, it didn't take long for the four to start joking around.

While his two friends had a short side conversation, Art took the opportunity to slip a private moment in with Poppy.

"Hey, can you promise me something?"

"What's that?"

"Promise me you'll be at my wedding."

"I'm not gonna promise you that, bud. But I do promise you that I'll try my best."

"That's all I ask."

Art wasn't planning on getting married anytime soon, but he had just started dating his first girlfriend. He was twenty-two when this conversation with Poppy happened.

*****

"Arthur? You still here?"

Art realized he was still holding Jimmy's hand under his.

"Yeah, sorry. I blanked for a second," he said as he let go of his granddad's hand.

"Thinking about anything in particular?"

"A lot, actually."

CHAPTER 9
Good Friends

Jimmy's viewing happened on a Sunday. A lot of his family and friends were there. A lot of people came to support Grandma. Everyone there knew Jimmy fairly well, except for two.

As the second viewing, the one after dinner, was about half way through, Art looked up at the long line of people and saw two of his best friends standing there.

At seventeen, he had only known Cookie and Wrecking Quinn for five years. They had met in junior high, seventh grade, when they were in the same class. They were the only two people who could make him laugh when he was in his darkest places.

Through the years, he always had their backs. When WQ's grandma died, Cookie and Art showed up to pay their respects. In the same manner that they made Art feel better, they did it for him.

When each went off to college, they continued to keep in touch. Cookie became a good friend to Inkspot, and Wrecking Quinn stopped by a few times to meet people like Xaviere and Spez.

Freshman year, Spez lost her father. It was the lowest she had ever been. Fran and Art dropped everything to be by her side in that tough time.

Fran lost her mom when she was still in high school. Her and Art went to Butler SHS together. She knew he was close with Cookie and WQ and enjoyed it when they visited LRC.

The older Art got, the more his friend groups intertwined. His Butler friends, LRC friends, work friends (summer camp, Target, etc.), and theater friends all started to blend into one big group.

Any time Poppy was in the hospital, his friends would check in on him. Some would reach out to others with whatever info they could get. It continued outside of Poppy. With his career, school choices, and even when he had his heart broken, they were always there for him.

Chapter 10

Grandma

Jimmy was still in the air force when some buddies invited him to have dinner in a bigger group. He was a little reluctant at first, but he decided to show.

There was a decent number of young women there too. He wasn't expecting that. He was so nervous that he might embarrass himself; he barely said a word all night.

At the end of the night, he was ready to get out of there. He had just stood up from his seat when one of the young women had already approached his side.

"Excuse me. You barely said anything all night. Who are you?"

"I'm, uh, Jimmy." He looked around for his friends, but they had all intentionally left the two alone.

"Hi, uh Jimmy." She chuckled. "You wanna go out some time? Just me and you?"

He really liked this one. At least from the little bit he got to know her that night. "Yeah."

"Great! Here's my number."

And just like that, she was gone.

*****

"So she asked you out?"

"I'm a little embarrassed to say that I was nervous."

"And you were still serving?"
"Not for much longer."

*****

"Jimmy, I really like you, but I can't continue to date you like this. Constantly wondering if you'll make it home safe or not," she said into her phone.

"Then I'll quit," he responded from the other end of the line.

"What?"

"I'll quit! I'll find something else to do."

"I can't ask you to do that." She was secretly hoping he would anyways.

"I've got a buddy working for Heinz 57. I'll talk to him tomorrow."

"But what about the air force?"

"My time serving ends soon, and I wasn't ready to sign up for more years anyways."

"Jimmy, are you sure you want to do this?"

"Of course. I'd do anything for you."

"That's really sweet."

*****

"She was worth it."

"But how exactly did she change your life?"

"Are you not listening?" Jimmy laughed.

"I am. I just don't see the connection here."

"Well then, let me continue."

*****

Jimmy and his love were enjoying themselves on a date. They had his place to themselves, and he made dinner for her. Just as they finished up, he dropped some news on her.

"They're really making you move to Mexico City?"

"If I want to stay with the company, yes."
"So what does that mean for us?"
"I was hoping you would tell me." Jimmy pulled a ring out of his pocket and got on one knee. "So what do you say? Will you marry me?"

She stopped and thought for a second. "What's for dessert?"

Jimmy gulped. "What?"

"What's for dessert?"

He stood up, put the ring back in his pocket, and went into the kitchen. A moment later, he stepped out with a tray of flan. He set it on the table for her.

She took a bite as she thought. She had been engaged before to someone she wasn't in love with, but she really liked Jimmy. *He cooks. Dessert too. He cleans. He has a great job. He took that job for me. What am I waiting for?*

"Yes."

"What?"

"Yes, Jimmy. I'll marry you."

Jimmy smiled, pulled the ring back out, put it on her hand, and kissed her.

"I've never been happier," they said simultaneously as they looked into each other's eyes.

*****

"Waiting for an answer to my question, Granddad."

"Patience."

The day before Jimmy's thirty-first birthday, they tied the knot. She moved down to Mexico to be with him. A few weeks later, she had become pregnant with their first child.

September 16, a healthy baby boy was born. Patricio Eduardo was their oldest of three. Each born outside of the US. Two in Mexico, and one in Venezuela. Each with a Spanish name on their birth certificate. Each using an English name when they moved back to Pittsburgh.

"Wait, I get it now."

"You do? I still have a lot of stories to share, Arthur."
"You can, if you wish, but I have my answer."
"Let me continue."
"Please do."

Chapter 11

Stop

"Wow, Granddad, that was beautiful!" Art said as he whipped a happy tear from his face.

"You ever have anything like that?"

"The closest I've come yet was with my ex."

"Are you doing okay?" He could tell that Art was a little skeptical to talk about it.

"Yeah, I'm fine."

"You still have feelings for her?"

"Some. I don't think strong feelings like what I had ever fully go away, but it's just a very small part of my heart."

"Have you meet someone else yet?"

"A lot, but none of them have given me that special moment yet."

"What do you mean?"

"Well, Granddad, let me tell you."

*****

It was Art's last first day at LRC. He was helping the freshman move in as he did every year. This time, his friend DJ was helping him unload cars.

As the two walked to the parking lot for the hundredth time, they talked about their summer.

"So yeah, it wasn't easy, but I made the decision to give it to God. Let it happen when it happens, ya know?" Art said.

"Let go and let God as they say." DJ chuckled.

"Exactly." Art laughed back.

They stopped at a van to help someone. There were five or so people standing there, but they had a lot to unpack.

"Can we help you folks?" DJ inquired.

"Please," answered a mother.

"Consider it done." Art grabbed some stuff and followed as they walked and talked. Eventually, arriving at a room on the fourth floor.

"Thanks guys," the mother said as DJ and Art set everything down.

Art looked up for the first time and saw a beautiful young blonde woman on the other side of the room. Just as when Poppy was in the hospital, time stopped.

He had totally forgotten that everyone else was there. DJ, the kid who they moved in, the mom, even his soon-to-be friends, Big Red and Chocodle, had all vanished from his mind. It was as if Harmony was the only other person in the room with him.

Then, suddenly, reality set in.

"Well, DJ, we should go."

Everyone laughed at this awkward response to ten seconds of silence.

"Right behind ya."

*****

"So you're waiting for that again?"

"Trying to."

"Don't you get tired of waiting?"

"Patience."

Both laughed at the response as they both knew Art was teasing Jimmy a little for giving the same response just a few minutes ago.

Chapter 12

More School

"So what was grad school like? I never did it, but I considered it."

"Why didn't you?"

"Grandma and I ended up just auditing classes after I retired instead."

"Oh, neat. It was tough, but also a lot of fun."

"Why's that?"

"Well, it's grad school," Art laughed. "But it was a writing program. The first semester was a lot like high school, lectures and all, but the second semester and the second year was almost all writing, and it was so much fun."

"What all did you write?"

"Mostly plays, film scripts, and TV pilots, but we also did a little bit of everything else."

"That sounds like a lot of fun!"

"It was, but it also allowed me extra time to figure out what I wanted to do with my life."

"Which was what?"

******

"Professor, can I talk to you for a minute?"

"Come in."

Art opened the door to meet with Robert Benjamin in his office as they had planned a few days before.

"Thanks for meeting with me!"

"Of course, Arthur. You're not just a former student, but a good friend too."

"Thanks!"

"So what can I do for you?"

"I need some advice."

"On what?"

"Well, I've been thinking about my future, and the more I think about it, I see myself as either a campus minister or a college professor. I've had my bachelor's for almost a year now, and I could only get a part-time job, which isn't what I wanted."

"Ah, I see. You know I'm an assistant pastor and that my wife is a campus minister… That's why you came to me."

"That, and because I haven't seen you in a while."

"Well, let me start by saying that both fields are really hard to get into."

"I knew ministry was. I've already applied for the CCO twice."

"Yeah, I know. Dave told me."

Dave was a good friend to both, but he was also the current campus minister at LRC. Robert was only a year or two older than Dave.

"So he also told you that I didn't get it?"

"Either time?"

"I had an online interview with them the other day, but I was already told that it's not gonna work out."

"I'm sorry to hear that."

"It's okay. I think what I really miss is the adjustability of college schedules…which is why I'm leaning more toward being a professor."

"That's great! What would you want to teach?"

"Writing, maybe some film classes, but definitely at LRC if possible."

"You know, they were just made into a university, so they might need more staff."

"That's right. It's LRU now. I keep forgetting that!"

"It's hard to adjust to it. And I don't just mean the name change."

"But I think I can adjust to being a professor."

INTERVIEWING GRANDDAD

"Good! If you think you can do it, I believe in you."

*****

"Professor, can I talk to you for a minute?"

"Come in."

Cindy opened the door to see Professor Arthur (as he had his students call him) sitting at his desk, writing his next project, and listening to Quinn XCII to get him in the zone.

"Thanks for meeting with me, Professor."

"What can I do for you, Cindy?"

"Can I ask your opinion on my project?"

"Sure." He turned the music down just as it switched to Marianas Trench. "But you already know what I'm gonna say, don't you?"

"No. Well, yes, but I just want to ask you something."

"Go ahead."

"I'm thinking about writing it as a short story, but I have a lot to write. Not enough to fill a full novel though."

"Have you ever heard of a BookShot or a novellete?"

"No."

"Well, they are both basically the same thing. A shorter version of a novel."

"Okay, so you're okay with me writing a long short story."

"Cindy, you know I only have two rules in my class, right?"

"Yes."

"What are they?"

"Be original, and trust your gut."

"It doesn't matter what I think of your final project as long as you follow those two rules and you're happy with it. That's all that matters. And remember that this is just your first final draft, it doesn't have to be perfect until you say it is."

"Thanks, Professor. I'll see you tomorrow."

"My door is always open, Cindy. Feel free to stop by anytime."

As she left, he turned his music back up to hear MAX and then he continued writing his first draft of his current project.

*****

"So that's why you have so many personal projects? All that free time."

"I'm only teaching a few classes a week. I spend the rest of my time writing, with my family, and I still work at Target on Saturdays."

"Still? After all these years?"

"Okay, I went back to Target after a few years off."

"A few years?"

Art ignored his granddad's question.

"Question 3: what kind of an impact did you leave while you were alive?"

"You could probably answer that better than I could."

"But I don't want to."

Chapter 13

After All These Years

Grandma looked down at the necklace around her neck, the same one she had been wearing every day for the last eight years. This wasn't just any old necklace, but rather her engagement ring, her wedding ring, and Granddad's wedding ring all three connected by the diamond. It meant the most to her.

"Mom, are you ready to go?"

Aunt S was helping Grandma move out of her house. The same house that Granddad had left eight years prior. The same house that she had lived in with him for eight years before he left.

"Yeah, sweetie, I'm ready."

As she left the house, knowing it was going to her son who spent thirty-plus years in the army and his family, she stopped in the yard. Not too far from the road sat a butterfly garden, one that was put there in Granddad's memory. "I'm gonna miss this place."

"I know, Mom. I know."

Both got in the car and drove to Grandma's new place.

Art was feeling lonely.

At the age of twenty-five, he was still living with his parents. He was also in his last semester of grad school. Everything seemed to stop when he realized he was single at an age where, just a few years ago, he hoped to be engaged by now.

One night, when things were really tough, he looked to his right and saw a bunch of pictures of him and Granddad from their trip to Europe. He smiled as he realized that their lives shared similarities.

*****

"Oh? So you mean to tell me that my impact only lasted a decade after I was gone?"

For the first time all day, Arthur could see that Jimmy was down.

"No, Granddad, that's not what I'm saying at all!"

"Then what are you saying?"

"I'm saying that your impact was so big it stayed with us for years after."

"Yeah…ten years."

"Much longer than that."

"It doesn't feel like it."

Arthur could tell that Jimmy was showing the depressed side of himself for the first time in years.

"Hang on. I want to show you a few things."

Jimmy started to tear up. "Like what?"

Art, for the first time all day, pulled his phone out of his pocket.

"Grab the notebook and flip to page 23. While you do that, I need to look through my pictures for a few things."

Jimmy grabbed the book that had been sitting between the two men and did just what his grandson said. When he flipped to the correct page, this is what he saw:

My Own Personal Guardian Angel

Everybody has one as I'm sure you've heard
With wings, a glow, and halo, they live up with the birds
But mine is very special 'cause we have spoken words
In a way, I'll tell you, we were both young nerds
And mine is always with me though not as some may seem
Hanging on my bedroom wall since I was just thirteen

INTERVIEWING GRANDDAD

On days I really need them, I look over and lean
For mine is my old granddad, who I saved on my screen.

And with that last line, Jimmy looked back at his grandson. "I don't get it. What do you mean I'm on your screen?"

Art turned his phone toward his grandfather. "You see this picture? It was taken a few months before you died, remember? Christmas 2012… Okay, so maybe it was closer to a year before, but I digress, that's not my point."

"Yeah, I remember that day. But what does that have to do with—"

"I've been carrying this photo on my phone for years now. I have a photo collage full of you and I on our trip to Switzerland and Austria from 2008." Art paused. "And I have this."

As Art reached into his pocket, he pulled out Grandma's necklace.

"Why do you have that?"

"When Grandma passed, it was the only thing I wanted."

Jimmy was smiling again. "Wow, that's amazing."

"No, what's amazing, Granddad, is that people still think about you every day. Em and I talk about you all the time. We never forgot you because you were unforgettable…no matter how busy I, I mean we, got."

"Okay, so there's your answer to number 3."

"Yeah." Art chuckled. "I guess so."

"And I know you'll never forget me. I just don't want you to lose your roots."

"That'll never happen, Granddad."

The two sat in silence for a brief moment while staring into each other's eyes.

"Now it's my turn to ask you something."

"What is it, Granddad?"

"Is this notebook full of personal projects?"

Chapter 14

A Collection of Letters

Hurting

It's tiring, knowing that at times all I feel like is a servant or a fool who is only meant to be called when someone needs something. Never hearing a ring unless they need a go for. What's worse is that tone in the voice. You know the one. It's the one that says, "Hey, buddy" in an "I need you to do something for me" kind of way, and not an "I missed you" kind. These are the moments that break me.

What will you do when I'm not so close? When I'm miles away, or farther. When I'm in a different time zone for vacation...or permanently. What will you do then? Hope I spend all day driving to see you? Or fly to you? Because as much as I love you, it hurts me to feel like I'm just a slave to you.

You tell me that I'm not and that's not your intention, but that doesn't change how I feel. And it doesn't help when you tell me that you aren't doing that over and over because of the tone in your voice. The "you're-being-ridiculous" tone.

I never said you were doing that, but I did say that I felt like you were, and you got defensive instead of helping me figure it out. How does that help?

There it is again. The "everyone-has-to-be-better-than-everyone-else" mentality that I was raised in. The "well so-and-so is a good singer, but my *child is better," the "you can cook, but* Mom's *a better chef," the "My son got a girlfriend before* yours*" type of thoughts are not good for us at all.*

I love you! I really do! And I promise I will until the end of my days and beyond, but that doesn't mean my emotions will stay as one. Love is so many things. It's not just the four definitions that the Greeks gave us (the act of sex, romantic love, love for family/friends, love of an object…like a really good pizza). It's all those things and more.

Many emotions can be tied into one, like how I love spending time with you but hate that you mostly talk about work. Or how I'm happy to hear your voice but sad when it's the first time in a while.

So yes, I love you! I've loved you for as long as I can remember, and I always will love you! I can say it a thousand times over again. I love you! I love you! I love you! *But all I need to do is say it once and you believe me, no matter what the actions were surrounding it. And I tell you every night when you are sleeping, as I head to bed myself, that I love you. Even when we are apart, I still remember that I love you.*

The pain is on my part, and it's something I must work on, which is why I'm writing now… to remind myself that you love me too…which I already know through the tears in your eyes as you read this, that you do!

Hurting (Part 2)

He tells me that he loves me, and I know that he does. I have no doubt in my mind about it! That being said, there are moments where it feels like the one I love more than life itself doesn't love me back as much and it kills me.

I believe that he tells me he loves me every night when I'm asleep. I don't doubt that one bit. And I know that he feels bad when he loses his temper or reacts poorly to a situation.

The thing that scares me, though, is that I feel like I don't know him anymore. It's partially because I barely see him, but it's also partially because he is more like his father every day.

The two of them seem to have some kind of connection, where they can just tell when it's fine to make jokes and when it's not fine too, which has lowered their disagreements a lot.

Now, I don't know who I am to either of them anymore. It scares me, and it has me thinking, Would he really move far away? I hope not, but even if he does, I know he's just a phone call away.

The problem is I'm really busy. Working seven days a week with not a lot of free time. When I do have free time, I'm tired. I want to call him to just say hi, but I'll see him again soon…or so I hope.

And sometimes I feel like they're both mad at me for working so much while they both see each other a little bit more, but I don't know.

Being the oldest isn't easy. I know that he knows that, and his father knows that. All this pressure to succeed, either from your parents or from yourself… or both.

The worst is when it's coming from both, and we all three know that. So that's at least one thing we all have in common. That, and our love for one another. And the good news is, that love we share takes all the negative feelings away as long as we let it.

INTERVIEWING GRANDDAD

Hurting (Part 3)

For the longest time, I didn't think anyone else quite understood me. My parents, or at least my mom, says that we have the same personality and that's why we butt heads a lot. My dad and I handle our frustrations the same way.

I never felt like I did enough for them, despite how much I love them. And now one of them is gone, and I just seem to disagree with my mother so much more.

And then there's my wife and son, who both work a lot. My wife I barely see despite living in the same house and sharing a bed. My son, I see a little more, mostly when we are watching TV together.

I guess he understands how my brain works, or at least more than anyone else does, but he won't be home forever, and that'll take me back to square one.

Here's the bright side: love. Yes, you've heard it before: "Love don't cost a thing." And that's true, that love is the best we can give someone.

I love my family very much—my wife, my son, my side of the family, my in-laws. I would go to bat for any of them, if the need be, even if it's against someone else I love.

Love makes us do crazy things, like wait five years until you have a child of your own, or be terrified of what may happen after you watch your child and your wife lose the ability to breath on their own. Sitting there in silence, fear in your heart.

But love is most amazing when it comes from Our Father, who lets them both live and lets them come home with me, who made it possible for our families to be there with me, who loves me so.

Love, my dear family, will always overpower the anger or the sorrow or the frustration I feel from not feeling like enough, and I know that it will help you too!

Hurting (Part 4)

I feel alone all the time. I know I'm not alone, but I feel it. I'm scared of being left alone and no one coming to check on me. It's terrifying.

My kids and grandkids are all growing up, and ever since you left me, I don't know how to feel. You're in a better place, reunited with your parents and mine, but I still miss you.

I'm afraid I'm pushing them away. They don't visit as much as they used to because they've all got school and jobs and other things, but it still has me petrified that I may die and nobody would know for a few days.

They're lucky! Having her entire side of the family no more than a twenty-minute drive away. Yes, a few of their children got married and moved across the country, but they still talk to them a few days a week. I wish our family was still that close.

What's that? They are? Of course they are, just not physically. It's okay that they aren't next door as long as they have each other.

They do? Of course, they do. They've been much closer since we all lost you…since I lost you.

The love we share, our family of thirteen, whose hearts were broken permanently that day you left us, will always hold us together.

I love them very much, and I would do anything for them. They know that.

INTERVIEWING GRANDDAD

You are gone for now, but one day, we will be reunited; and when that day comes, my heart won't be broken anymore.

Love is a four-letter word. Just like life, wife, kids, move, home, and over. And just like all these other words, love will last forever!

Jimmy put the notebook down after a moment.
"Well, what do you think?"
"Those were beautiful."
"Thanks!"
A brief silence.
"What's question 4?"
"Granddad, we've been doing this all afternoon. Why don't we take a break and come back to it later?"
"Yeah, maybe that's for the best."
Art grabbed the notebook and moved it to the other side of him before scootching next to Jimmy.
"Hey, are you getting hungry?"
"I don't need to eat anymore, remember?"
"Right, sorry, it's been a while since we've hung out."
"Yeah, because you've been busy."
"But never too busy for you."
Art smiled at Jimmy before attempting to lean his head down on his grandfather. Somehow, Art didn't fall through the ghost next to him as if Jimmy had briefly been human again.

The two sat this way for a while as they watched the sun slowly set.

Chapter 15

Years of Fear

Arthur woke up in a panic. Sweat beaded all over his body as his heart raced as fast as a member of the Indy 500. He looked over and realized that Jimmy was gone.

As he looked throughout the graveyard for his grandfather, he noticed more graves popping up around him.

Jennifer.
Zachary.
Ernie.
Bobbie.
Pauline.
Amy.
Patrick.
Emily.
Tim.
Adam.
Tray.
Connor.
Johnny.
Nancy.
Quinn.
Kristen.
Jessica.
"Stop!"
Mollie.
Jeffrey.

INTERVIEWING GRANDDAD

Olivia.
"Stop!"
Samuel.
Savannah.
Madison.
"Stop! Stop! S<small>TOP</small>!"

More graves continued to pop up around him. He stood up to run away but couldn't move. The bench he had been sitting on disappeared. The notebook fell to the ground and flipped open to the last page.

The page was blank at first, but as Arthur kept looking at it, it filled itself in his handwriting.

> *Goodbye. I love you. Hugs and kisses. I'll see you soon. Goodbye! I love you! Hugs and kisses, and I'll see you soon! Goodbye, I love you! Hugs and kisses, and I'll see you soon! Goodbye, I love you! Hugs and kisses, and I'll see you soon! I'll see you soon! I'll see you soon! I'll see you* soon!

The notebook fell into a small hole in the ground. The hole continued to grow, and Art fell in it too. A gravestone popped up that said *Arthur Parts, 1996–?*

Suddenly, Art was surrounded by his loved ones. Each in all black, and with tears in their eyes, they started piling dirt on top of him.

"Hey! H<small>EY</small>!"

But nobody could hear him.

"Help!"

*****

"Arthur, wake up."

Art jumped awake and saw that the night sky was speckled in twinkling stars. He sat up, looked over at his grandfather, and sighed.

"Are you okay, Arthur?"

"I'm fine. Just a nightmare."

Jimmy smiled.

"How long was I out?"

"Just a few hours."

Arthur checked his phone—10:07 p.m., no missed calls, seven unread messages.

"Oh boy, I should probably head home."

"It's getting late, Arthur. Why don't you stay here tonight?"

Art took a look around and was relieved to see that the graveyard had returned to the way it was when he got there.

"Yeah, maybe I will." Art smiled.

"What was your nightmare about?"

"Just a recurring thing I keep having."

Jimmy responded as if he knew the answer. "It's not as scary as you'd think."

"What isn't?"

"Dying."

"That's not the part that bothers me."

"The pain is only temporary."

Art looked up at his grandfather and let out a little smirk. "Things haven't changed since you left."

"Well, I hope that's not true!"

Art laughed. "No, I mean, you've always been able to tell what I'm thinking."

"I know what you meant, Arthur, but a lot of other things have changed."

"Well, yeah. I have a bachelor's and a master's degree, I've been in relationships, and I've lost my three little fur babies."

"Yeah, that's all true, but I meant that you aren't living in constant fear anymore."

Art paused. "You…you knew about that?"

"Of course I did, considering I was the reason it happened."

"It's not your fault. I just became more precautious."

"Arthur, it's hard to be precautious when it's not your life."

"I know, but I was so worried about them."

"Worried about who?"

INTERVIEWING GRANDDAD

"You know the answer to that."

"Yes, but I want to hear you say it out loud."

Art closed his eyes and recited a few prayers similar to one he would have said a lot in his teenage years or early twenties.

"Dear God, please stay with Nanny and Poppy. They are both nearing eighty, and I worry about them, especially with Nanny's heart and Poppy's body weakened by cancer."

"Go on."

"Dear God, please stay with Grandma as she nears eighty. I know that's when her husband left, and I worry it will happen with her too."

"Keep going."

"Dear God, please stay with J and Z after the wreck, and please help them become parents. Dear God, please stay with Mom and Dad. Please help me to not damage my relationship with them as I get older and learn more lessons. Dear God, please stay with me."

Jimmy paused for a moment as he watched his grandson starting to tear up.

"Hey, it's okay. They worked."

CHAPTER 16

How Much Longer?

"Did they?"

"Of course, they did. J and Z are parents, aren't they?"

"Yeah, but—"

"Sometimes prayers get answered in ways we don't want them to, but they're still answers."

Art stood up and started to walk away. "I need something to eat. I haven't had food in twelve hours."

"Okay, fair enough, but it's the middle of the night."

"I'll find something. Just might have to drive for a bit."

Jimmy smiled.

"I'll be back soon. I promise that I won't leave you for good."

"I know you won't."

Arthur got in his car and started to drive off. As he drove out of sight, some familiar faces made their way to Jimmy.

Art grabbed his coffee and sandwich from the drive-through window, said thanks, and pulled into a nearby parking spot so that he could eat without any issue.

"Art, is that you?"

As he looked up, he saw the face of his ex-girlfriend staring at him. He reluctantly rolled his window down.

"Hey, lady. How have you been?" he asked, despite being uncomfortable.

Before she could answer, he noticed the engagement ring on her finger.

"I've been pretty good."

"That's good, I guess."

As she felt the awkward tension, she tried to break it. "I miss you, you know!"

"You're the one that dumped me, remember?"

Art was tired, hungry, and frustrated. He didn't care if he was nice anymore, aside from still having a very small part of her still in his heart.

"We've talked about this. We drifted apart."

"Bullshit. You pushed me away!"

"Because I felt like I was losing you."

"Then why didn't you talk to me?"

"I tried to."

"So you're blaming me?"

Art looked up and saw her beautiful smile for the first time in years. "I'm sorry. I'm just in the middle of something. I've got to go." He rolled his window up, quickly ate his sandwich, and drove off.

On his way back to the graveyard, he couldn't stop thinking to himself, *Why does she get to be happy while I'm still miserable? When will it be my time? Why am I still single?*

As he continued to drive, he wrote a new poem in his mind (transcribed to paper later).

Patience Isn't Easy

P is for pathetic as I've been called before
A is for annoying, antsy, or asshole
T is for trying, maybe a bit too hard
I is for irritating, indecisive, or insecure
E is for everyone's friend, but no one's love
N is for not now, and I've had enough
C is for crazy, only jokers in his cards
E is for endless nights with feelings of being unsure

Patience isn't easy
And I've prayed every day
For help to fix these feelings

And send me on my way
"Be confident, and girls will notice"
"Focus on yourself for the right reasons"
"Life's too short to wait, but it's also too short to worry"
"Before you know it, you'll be married"

P is for praying that an answer comes one day
A is for allow God to help you in every way
T is for tomorrow, or the next day, or the next
I is for it will all be okay
E is for enjoy each day and hope for all the best
N is for now He just wants you to rest
C is for compatibility with little or no subtext
And E is for even though it might not feel like it, even when you're down, even when the world is going on normally…you just have to pray

CHAPTER 17

These Dreams

Jimmy noticed his grandson returning about an hour after he left. For the first time in a long time, he panicked.

"All right, everyone. I'll ask him about it. But for now, you all need to scatter. He'll break down if he knows you're all here."

The familiar faces that had surrounded Jimmy went their separate ways—out of sight and sure that Arthur didn't see them as he pulled into a parking spot and walked back to the same bench Jimmy had been sitting on all day.

"Well, I feel a little better."

"Good, I'm glad you were able to find a place open this late."

"You and me both."

"Arthur, can I ask you something?"

"Always."

Jimmy took a moment to carefully orchestrate his choice of words so that he didn't upset Art but also in a way that he would be able to ask the question that was on his mind.

"Are you doing okay?"

Arthur wasn't upset by this question at all, but he was curious as to why it took his granddad a few seconds to ask it when he had been asking far worse all day.

"Um…yeah, I am. Why?"

"I know about your struggles. You've always had a minor obsession with women… Some might even call it an addiction. I also know that you haven't felt yourself for the last few years."

"What are you getting at?"

Jimmy took a deep breath. "Arthur, I love you just the way you are, but I also know that you've been hurting a lot, especially mentally, over these last two years."

Art began melting down in a way he only did with his close friends for the last five or so years of his life. "About two years ago, it all started when Elmo died. A few weeks later, it was Mittens, and a few months after that, it was Nacho Kitty. Losing my three feline fur babies broke me…but as I'm sure you know, that was just the start of it."

"Go on."

"J and Z's accident, grad school, starting a new job… And that was all in the same week." Art could barely contain himself anymore.

"I'm listening, Arthur. Keep going."

"The break up really hit close to home."

"Why was that?"

"Because I was practically twenty-two when I finally fell in love, and it was over before I even turned twenty-four."

Jimmy didn't want to break his grandson, but he could tell that Art was bottling a lot of emotions up in order to protect them both.

"You're not mentioning one of them."

"Do I have to, Granddad?"

"No, you don't *have* to, but I think it would help."

"Okay, well, you already know, so I might as well say it. Grandma and Poppy both turned eighty within that time."

"And that bothered you because?"

"Because…that's how old you would have been…if you had lived another few months."

Arthur could barely get the last sentence out.

"Arthur, most of these things were out of your control. Why take all this on your shoulders?"

Art had to take a few seconds. As he wiped the tears away, he composed himself the best that he could. "Because the one thing that was in my control, the relationship, well, I let that end."

Jimmy reached out and put his hand on Art's shoulder. Just like earlier, Jimmy felt solid for a few brief moments. "Any relationship, romantic or not, is a two-way street." He smiled at his grandson. "It wasn't your fault."

INTERVIEWING GRANDDAD

Fighting, Fighting, Fighting

People you love are always there to share something with you
But that is only true if those you love, love you back too
So take a stand and help them out no matter what they do
'Cause even if you argue, you can start out like anew

Against them, for them, with them are the types that do exist
Sometimes they coincide but only if they top your list
Of those who matter most to you, of that I must insist
But they're the ones who care the most and never will resist

Arguments can happen verbally but just be careful
Physical is terrifying when there's much to handle
"Emotional abuser," says the plaque that's on their mantle
Then that's the time to leave them off with nothing left but candle

"I saw her first, so that means that I called dibs"
Sounds like something from the mouth of teeny, tiny little kids
Remember not to let someone spread rumors, lies, or fibs
And know that words may never hurt like gut punches in the ribs

I mean really, what's the point guys? When life is just so short
We should always have each other in a friendly, fun cohort
So remember these last words from me, which I will not abort,
We can always have each other if we give into the sort

Chapter 18

All Goodbyes Hurt

"You've really grown up since the last time I saw you. I mean that. You're much more responsible for your own actions now, and you've matured so much."

"Granddad... I really haven't."

"Of course you have! Why would you say that?"

"Because I'm still a scared little kid on the inside."

As the last tear left Arthur's eye, he saw Granddad smiling in anticipation.

"It's like when I was a kid, and Nanny would have me walk over the grates on the sidewalk even though she knew I was terrified of falling in."

"She was just trying to help you face your fears."

"Or what about when I had a seizure in my sleep, and I couldn't see anything for hours. Unsure of where I was or who was there as I slowly regained consciousness."

"I was there. You know Grandma and I dropped everything to come and check on you and keep an eye on your parents. Nanny and Poppy were there too. And even those that weren't there kept praying that you would make it out of that hospital okay."

"What about my personal hell that was my twenty-third year?"

"That one is a lot harder to explain."

"I lost all three of my boys. All three of my furry feline brothers passed away within months of each other, and that's when I had no choice but to grow up."

"Arthur—"

"And of course J and Z were in their car accident that year."

"Please listen—"

"And my breakup and Poppy and Grandma's eightieth birthdays."

"You survived that year, and you became an amazing person with a ton of new friends! You persevered, and now look at you, you're amazing. I love you!"

*****

Jimmy was seventy-nine when he walked out of his house on the day he left his family. It was a few months before his birthday. As he was getting ready for the day, and his wife slept peacefully, he got a call he wasn't quite ready to answer.

"Hello?"

"It will only take a minute."

As he left his bathroom, he walked over to his wife and kissed her on the forehead.

"I love you so much!"

She opened her eyes and saw that the bathroom door was still closed.

"Jim, honey, is everything all right?"

No answer.

As she got out of bed, he watched her from the window.

"I'm so sorry."

As he left, she opened the bathroom door and was saddened to see the message he had left for her.

*****

"Even if that's true, even if I did survive it all, I still was forced to grow up, and it wasn't fair."

"Life isn't always fair, Arthur. Look at how I ended up here."

"Can we please not talk about that?"

"Why not?"

"Please!" Arthur stood up and threw the notebook down in a moment of angst. It flipped open to the first page.

"What's that?"

Art looked down and quickly back up again. "It's something I wrote years ago. It was a way for me to grieve."

"Can I read it?"

"Yeah, sure. Go ahead."

At Childhood's End

One year ago
I lost my best friend
My fat, brat cat
At childhood's end

Orange and fluffy
With claws that could kill
He put up a fight
Till his very last will

For a final few days
He barely would move
Just lost lots of blood
As he set his own groove

And now he's beyond
Any space or time
Reunited with brothers
Both furry, both mine

And the three of them sit there
No need to pretend
That they hated each other
(As cats take a stand)

INTERVIEWING GRANDDAD

No alpha males here
While they watch me pour out
My once innocent heart
Full of pity and doubt

But I know that I'll see them
At some time again
Years off in the future
When my time will end

And the sad truth behind it
I'll leave new best friends
As a watch them tear up
At childhood's end

Chapter 19

We Are Not Monsters

"*Look around, Ted. You're all alone.*"

"What?" Jim had just put the notebook down.

"Sorry, I was quoting one of my favorite shows."

"Oh, yeah. What's it about?"

"It was a show about a guy telling his kids the long and winding road that led to him meeting their mother." A brief pause. "It's one of my favorites because I can relate to it so well."

Jimmy smiled. "Can I tell you a secret? Something I've never told anyone before."

"Of course you can, Granddad."

"This is a little embarrassing, but before I met Grandma, I never thought I would meet anyone either."

"It's a cliché."

"It's a cliché, but it's true."

Arthur laughed. "I can relate."

"Maybe so, but you did find someone eventually, right?"

"Right."

"And you didn't even have to look that hard. I mean, you only have one ex, right?"

"Correct…but I sure did a lot of searching before and after her."

"I'm sure you did. Actually, I know you did. And you were never alone."

"Well, I was. I was single for a while."

"Single and alone are not the same thing."

INTERVIEWING GRANDDAD

Art thought back to his early twenties for a few moments.

*****

It was June of his twenty-third year on this planet. He was working at a summer camp when he got a call just a few weeks in.

"Big Red, how's New Jersey?"

"Not great," said the voice on the other end. "I got dumped today."

At the end of the summer, Art met with Big Red almost immediately.

"I really thought that she was the one man," Big Red said as tears ran down her face.

"Listen to me, you are not a bad person."

"But I feel like a monster."

Art smirked as he held on to Big Red with all of his might. "Did I ever tell you about a similar moment I had with X?"

"No."

X was one of Art's roommates in college. They started as acquaintances before becoming best friends. From sophomore to senior year, they stuck together like peanut butter and the roof of a mouth.

At the start of their junior year, Art was told that "his attitude needed to change or he was getting kicked out" by one of their other roommates.

"Hey, X?" The two sat alone in the living room.

"Yes?"

"Am I a monster?"

"No! You aren't. And I don't want you thinking that you are."

"But—"

"But nothing. You are not a horrible person. He's overreacting, and you deserve to know that I will stick by your side no matter what."

"Thanks, buddy. I love you!"

"I love you too, man."

*****

"You're right, Granddad. I was never alone."

"Of course I'm right. I know everything [that I want to]."

"But it really did feel desperate at moments."

"Like when?"

"Like when I was twenty-five, and I told a girl I liked her but then messed it all up just a few months later."

"How did you mess it up?"

"I said something that I shouldn't have, and it ruined our friendship."

"But you were friends, so you must have had some good moments."

Art smiled. "Like when I sent her that letter."

> *It's been over a year now since my ex dumped me, and it took me a while to feel like myself again.*
>
> *Let me explain the best way I know how…in writing.*
>
> *There's this beauty that I met at my job. For the first year that I worked there, we barely talked, but when we did, I could sense that she was a very genuine person. And then suddenly, around the same time she was added to a group chat I'm a part of, my eyes were opened.*
>
> *Here's the crazy thing, she has some similarities to my ex. (When I noticed them, they were both eighteen. They went to the same high school. They were both in marching band with my best friend, Big Red. And weirdly enough, they both have the initials MZ.) Here's the crazier thing, my coworker saved me from myself without even doing anything.*
>
> *There are people who might judge me, with our decent age gap, and a ton more that would judge me for (I guess you could call it crushing) on a high-school senior.*
>
> *So, M***, if you ever get the chance to read this, let me start off by saying, "thank you." Thank*

you for being the friendliest person I know! Thank you for giving me hope again! And thank you for being the reason that I truly feel myself again!

And yes, I do like you. I don't know if I'll do anything about it, 1 percent because of the above societal reasons and 99 percent because I have a lot of bags to carry as it is. But let me ask you this: Can you tell that I've been "attempting to" flirt with you this last week or so?"

"Wow. What else did you do right?"

Looking Good, Feeling Great

I don't think I've felt this upbeat in a while
Walking around, showing my smile
Doing what I would call dressing up
Just because I want to

Most people would be sad after the events of yesterday
But I feel bittersweet, and that's the most I'll say
I didn't know I would feel so conflicted
When I told her how I felt, I didn't feel restricted

I finally feel like myself again
And it's partially because I was rejected by a friend
Not a pinch of anger, not a sign of embarrassment
Yet I'm terrified, due to my impatience

It'll happen one day. Yes, I know it will
It could be tomorrow or a thousand days off still
And just like Trevor Daniel and Selena sang in strife
"Last night was the last night of my past life"

So I'll keep doing my best to truly be myself
While working even harder to show everyone else

That even when you're lonely, you aren't really alone
Just show some confidence in how you act and in your clothes

Jim smiled as Art finished reading the poem.

"See how you were able to learn from your mistakes, even so close to your awful year?"

"Yeah, I guess."

"What was it your friend MorganDoor said when you were down?"

"How do you know MorganDoor?"

"That's not important. What did she say?"

"She said, 'We've all done crappy stuff, that doesn't make you a crappy person.'"

"Arthur, you're not a monster. You never were, and you never will be. You, my sweet grandson, are human."

Chapter 20

Thirteen Broken Hearts

Art looked up at Jim and noticed that he appeared to be fading away.

"Granddad? What's happening?"

"It seems that my twenty-four hours are almost up."

"What? What do you mean?"

"I have to go back to heaven soon."

Art looked at his watch. Sure enough, it had been twenty-three hours and fifty-five minutes, approximately, since they had started their reunion.

"How much longer do we have?"

"Five minutes."

Art started to cry. "But I don't want you to go."

"I know, but I have to."

"I've really missed you!"

"You can always come back and visit me again."

"But, Granddad—"

"You've been busy, but you made the time to see me today, so I know you can do it again."

"That's not it."

"Then what is it?

Four minutes. Art seemed to be frozen still. "Well…"

Arthur sat there, unsure how to ask his grandfather the final question.

"What is it?"

Art looked down at the notebook and opened it to the last page. He saw his list of questions. They had all been answered, but one.

Three minutes.

"Arthur, are you okay?"

Art took the pen out of his pocket and crossed out the unanswered question. Behind the pen smudge were the words "why did you leave on the day you died?"

"Yeah, I'm here. I'm okay."

"Are you sure? You zoned out for a moment?"

"I know. I'm sorry."

"Is there anything else you want to talk about before I go?"

"No, there's not."

"Are you sure?"

"Yeah." A pause. "Can we just sit here? Be in each other's company for a few."

"Sure."

Two minutes.

*****

Jimmy's alarm woke him up at 8:00 a.m. It was August 20, 2013.

As he followed his usual Tuesday morning routine: showering, shaving, changing into his tennis gear, he got a call that he wasn't quite ready to answer.

"Hello?"

"James, this is Peter."

"Is it time to go?"

"I'm afraid it is."

"Let me say goodbye to my wife first."

"You have to go. Now."

"It'll only take a minute."

As he left his bathroom, he walked over to his wife and kissed her on the forehead.

"I love you so much!"

She opened her eyes and saw that the bathroom door was still closed.

"Jim, honey, is everything all right?"

INTERVIEWING GRANDDAD

No answer.

As she got out of bed, he watched her from the window. A skylight window.

"I'm so sorry."

As he left, she opened the bathroom door and was saddened to see the dead body that had left for her.

She ran for the phone as quickly as she could.

"Everything will be okay, my child."

*****

"Granddad, did you say something?"

One minute.

"No, I don't think I did."

Behind the two stood the familiar faces Jimmy had spoken with just hours before. Art had no idea that his mother, father, grandparents, other relatives, friends, and pets had all shown up during the night. They were also all fading away.

"Granddad, I love you and the others so much. Can you do me a favor?"

"What's that, Arthur?"

"Can you tell them all that I think about them a lot? Just like I do with you."

"Of course I can."

"Thanks!"

Thirty…

Twenty-nine…

Twenty-eight…

Twenty-seven…

Twenty-six…

About the Author

Andre Parker is from Butler, Pennsylvania. As an only child, his family was always important to him (which is why he has always felt close to them). Becoming very outgoing when he was ten, Andre started opening up to those who would become his closest friends. Now, with a bachelors from La Roche University in Communications and a masters from Point Park University in writing for the stage and screen, he has found a love for writing in his late high school and college careers.

Hoping to teach or act, Andre continues to write as a form of therapy and a way to share his stories with others. Andre has also acted in state theater and short films in his free time as well as spending as much time with his family and friends as possible.

CPSIA information can be obtained
at www.ICGtesting.com
Printed in the USA
BVHW040240070622
639108BV00005B/83